MW01141176

THE WORLD'S SHORTEST JOKES

by
Buster Gutt

NEW MILLENNIUM PRESS
Beverly Hills

ISBN: 1-893224-97-X

Library of Congress Cataloging-in-Publication Data Available

Text Design: Kerry DeAngelis, KL Design

New Millennium Press
301 North Canon Drive
Suite 214
Beverly Hills, CA 90210

www.NewMillenniumPress.com

10 9 8 7 6 5 4 3 2 1

HOT

TOPICS

JOKES

Did you hear mogul
Ted Turner retired?
He wants to dedicate
more time to philandery—
I mean, philanthropy.

Did you see the new
musical about genetic
engineering?
Send in the Clones.

Did you hear producer
Phil Spector's girlfriend
cut a new record?
**It went to number one
with a bullet.**

Poor J. Clifford Baxter—
**He needed the Enron
scandal like he needed a
hole in the head.**

What's the difference
between FBI fugitive
Whitey Bulger and
Enron's Kenneth Lay?
**One's a thief and a con
man, and the other's
just a Mafia chief.**

How is ex-congressman James Traficant like a Holiday Inn? **They both occasionally get new rugs.**

How were scientists able to fill the hole in the ozone layer? **They plugged it with James Traficant's hair.**

Why was Monica Lewinsky promoted to the FBI? **For figuring out who Deep Throat was.**

What's Bill Clinton's favorite ballad? **"You Don't Send Me Flowers Anymore"**

Did you hear about the latest HMO to fail? **Killem Permanente**

Did you hear about the two priests who were so close **only an altar boy could come between them?**

The new education requirements for presidential interns are tough: **a degree at Oral Roberts, and a masters from Ball State.**

Some interns even get PhD's from Morehead State.

Arthur Andersen has been forced to work for *Playboy*—**I guess the rear ends justify the means.**

Have you read the new Playboy article on corporate mismanagement— **"Boobs of Enron"? And it didn't have a centerfold—just a spreadsheet.**

What's the liquid capacity of Monica Lewinsky's mouth? **One U.S. leader.**

Did Monica get a contract when she got her new government job? **No, just a handshake and an oral agreement.**

What's Enron's company motto? **"Take the Money Enron."**

Overheard priest pick-up line— **"You call that a confession?"**

What does
ENRON stand for?
**Employees Net
Return On Nothing**

Oh well, as they say
at Arthur Andersen:
**There's no accounting
for taste.**

Did you hear about the
congressman who got
in trouble for turning
over a new page?

What's the difference between Enron's pension plan and a pet rock? **One is a sham visited on an unsuspecting public, and the other is a novelty gift.**

Why did the congressional page quit his job in disgust? **He couldn't afford the kneepads.**

What do you call the Clinton administration?
Sex between the Bushes.

Why are Monica Lewinsky's cheeks so puffy?
She's withholding evidence.

What's a good way to bug Osama bin Laden?
Ask him, **"Didn't I see you last night at Hooters?"**

What's another way
to bug Osama?
**Reveal surprise
endings of _E.R._ and
Will and Grace.**

But what's the best
way to bug Osama?
**Remark that the last
time you saw a cave this
nice, Fred and Wilma
were living there.**

Did you see the new documentary on fishing in the Chesapeake Bay, *The Blair Fish Project?*

What do you call a lawyer gone bad?
A senator.

BEST OF AL QAEDA TV

Win Bin Laden's Money

Wheel of Fear and Fortune

Afghanistan's Funniest Home Executions

My Mullah The Car

Flog the Press

Married With 74 Children

Just Shoot Everything

My Favorite Martyr

Judge Omar

TeleTalibans

Cave and Garden TV

Trading Caves

Al Qaeda For a Day

TOP TEN PRIEST HITS

"Satisfaction (I Can't Get No...)"

"Red, Red Wine"

"You Can't Touch This"

"Beat It"

"Hand Jive"

"Smells Like Teen Spirit"

"I've Got the Whole World
In My Hands"

"I'm Too Sexy (For My Cloak)"

"They're Writing Psalms
of Love (But Not For Me)"

"Light My Friar"

RICH
AND
DEFAMOUS
JOKES

If the Barefoot Contessa married Danny DeVito, she'd be **Ina-Garten-DeVito**.

If director Ron Howard received a prize of Italian pastries, he'd be **Opie Won Cannolis**.

What's Michael Jackson's favorite movie?
Throw Momma and the Kids from the Train

If Lizzie Borden married jazz great Dizzie Gillespie, would she be Mrs. Dizzy Lizzie? **No, but she'd have great chops**.

What type of lighting does the *Oprah Show* use on Dr. Phil? **Dome lighting**

What do you call a daredevil in the Middle Ages? **Medieval Knieval**

Did you read the new book about the retiring sportscaster?
Far from the Madden Crowd

Have you heard Diana Ross' latest record, **_Stop! in the Name of the Law?_**

What's the difference between Joan Rivers and a crocodile?
One's an ancient amphibian with leathery skin, and the other is....oh, never mind.

Did you see Halle Berry's latest movie, ***Driving Miss Dizzy?***

If Barbra Streisand married gridiron great Lawrence Taylor, would she be **Mrs. BLT**?

If actress Jill Hennessy married Michael Jordan, would she be **Mrs. Crossing Jordan twice**?

Did you hear about Anna Nicole Smith's new reality series, ***American Idle?***

How come when *American Idol's* Simon Cowell's boat capsized the sharks refused to eat him?
Professional courtesy

How is Joan Rivers like ex-President Teddy Roosevelt?
They are both revered as rough riders.

What do you call a New Age show about cooking?
Yanni Can Cook

How is Britney Spears like ex-President Thomas Jefferson?
They are both reputed to be famous Virgin-ians.

What's the difference between Kurt Cobain and a pair of bright slacks?
One's a red Docker, and the other's a dead rocker.

What's the difference between Steven Seagal and Mount Rushmore?
They can put expressions on Mt. Rushmore.

What's the difference between the Osbournes and The Addams Family? **One is a frightening, dysfunctional bunch of weirdos, and the other is just creepy and kooky.**

What's the difference between Anna Nicole Smith and a blimp? **You can fit a blimp in a hangar.**

What's the difference between Anna Nicole Smith and a guided missile? **You can program a missile.**

How is Monica Lewinsky like a convention hall? **They both swallow up political speakers.**

Did you hear sailors had a raffle on their ship? **First prize was a picture of Anna Nicole Smith in a bathing suit. Second was a shot of her naked.**

What's the difference between Eminem and a horse? **You can train a horse to act.**

What's the difference between the Osbournes and a monkey cage? **You can teach monkeys sign language.**

Everyone in Hollywood is getting a hybrid car— **they'll save a lot of gas driving to their Lear jets**.

What's the difference between the kids on *The Real World* and a pet mascot? **Mascots have actually been to college campuses.**

What did the man cleaning elephant dung say when asked why he doesn't get another job? **"What? And give up show business?"**

Did you hear about the new morning talk-show spin-off: ***A Womb With A View?***

Why was Ozzy Osbourne kicked out of the PTA?
For always f****ing coming late to the f////*&& meetings.

Why won't Ozzy let his family watch reruns of *Leave it to Beaver?*
He doesn't like it when Ward spanks the Beaver.

No really.... Why won't Ozzie let his family watch *Leave it to Beaver?*
He thought June set a bad, f//****ng example.

What's Ward Cleaver's favorite time of the year? **When June comes.**

Did you hear about the new sitcom based on the Osbourne family, *Ozzie and Harridan?*

If the second *Lord of the Rings* movie does badly, will the third one be called *Faulty Towers?*

Did you see the new movie about the marriage of overweight computer operators, ***My Big Fat Geek Wedding?***

Did you see the new movie about Tonya Harding's comeback, ***The Lard of the Rinks?***

Why did Alex's choice on *The Bachelor* refuse to marry him?
She saw what was on the bottom of the hot tub.

What do you call the new show about prostitutes making their own movie? **HBO Project REDLIGHT**

Did you hear about the new teen comedy featuring Prince Harry— *Dude, Where's My Castle?*

And is that why Prince Harry insists on being called **"Your Highness"**?

Do you think Anne Boleyn ever received severance pay?

Did you hear about the new eco-friendly bakery in Hollywood: **Ed Bagel Jr's**?

What's the difference between Arnold Schwarzenegger and the Mona Lisa? **People claim the Mona Lisa can change expressions.**

How is Arnold Schwarzenegger like a cigar store Indian? **They both love a good smoke and act like they're made of wood.**

Why did Martha Stewart rush to get the chicken soup off the burner? **She got a tip the stock had shorted.**

Why were the brass at Xerox arrested? **For copying Leona Helmsley's tax returns.**

What's the difference between Martha Stewart and Leona Helmsley?
Leona knows how to bake a license plate.

What's Leona Helmsley's favorite movie?
Darby O' Gill and the Little People

Why does Martha love baking with cheese?
Because it's a Gouda thing.

Supposedly said by
Mae West when asked
if she got her furs and
jewels for being good:
**"Goodness had nothing
to do with it."**

What do you call it
when you come back
in the next life as
Billy Bob Thornton?
Reintarnation

How did Sydney Biddle
Barrows get started
in her business?
**By coming on the
Mayflower.**

Did Sydney Biddle Barrows
book first class passage
on the Mayflower?
**No, she worked her
way across.**

Why didn't anyone buy
Prince's last album?
No one could de-cypher it.

Why didn't Michael
Jackson make it as a
nanny?
**He threw out the baby
with the bathwater.**

Have you heard Michael's new torch song, **"Nobody Nose the Trouble I've Seen"**?

What did the hostess of the birthday party say when Winona Ryder left? **"Well, that takes the cake."**

When Winona Ryder left Malibu, did the shopkeepers find anything taken? **No, but Atlantis is still missing.**

If Anita Gillette married Ruben Blades, would she be **Mrs. Gillette-Blades**?

Did you hear about the hot new show on House and Garden Television? *Sex on the Settee*

What's Queen Latifah's favorite new movie? *Divine Secrets of the Yo-Yo Sisterhood*

If Ivana Trump married Armand Hammer, wouldn't she be **Ivana Hammer**?

If one of the King family sisters married Little Richard, would she be **Little King-Richard**?

Why didn't Rick James' girlfriend make it to his concert on time? **She was all tied up.**

No really—why didn't Rick James' girlfriend show up? **Beats me.**

Did you hear they've scheduled Emeril's wedding to take place on his show? The episode is called **"My Big Fat Grease Wedding."**

What's the difference between Roseanne Barr and the national deficit? **You can reduce the deficit.**

If Karen Black married Carrot Top, wouldn't she be **Mrs. Black-Top**?

What's the difference between Anna Nicole Smith and the national budget?
You can trim the budget.

How did Lady Di win at Clue?
She knew the butler did it.

What was Prince Charles' favorite spy flick?
Di Another Day

What was Lady Di's riding instructor's favorite TV show?
Father Knows Best

Did Hugh Grant enjoy his drive down Sunset Boulevard?
Yes, he thought it was Divine.

What's Elizabeth Hurley's favorite bar?
The Bada Bing

What do you call the film production company formed by a TV shrink? **Dr. PhilCo**

Supposedly Mae West said: "I love movies—I go to the Paramount all day, then Fox all night"...

LADIES
AND
GERMS
JOKES

Words you never want to hear when making love: **"Honey, I'm home."**

Why do black widow spiders kill their mates after mating?
To stop the snoring.

If praying mantises bite off their mates' heads after lovemaking, do they still refer to it as **"getting some tail"**?

I've been in love with the same woman for over 50 years, **and if my wife finds out, I'm dead**.

I take my girlfriend everywhere...
she just keeps finding her way back.

What do you call a man with half a brain?
Exceptional.

What's the difference between a man and government bonds?
Bonds mature.

What's the difference between a Porsche and a porcupine?
A porcupine has pricks on the outside.

What should a wife do if she finds her husband staggering in the backyard?
Shoot him again.

What do you call
an intelligent man
in America?
A tourist.

Why are men with
pierced ears more
prepared for marriage?
**They have already
experienced pain and
bought jewelry.**

Is a Swiss army knife
male or female?
**Male—has lots of uses
but spends most of its
time opening bottles.**

Kidneys—male or female?
Female—go to bathroom in pairs.

Auto tires—male or female?
Male—go bald and are over-inflated.

Hot air balloon—male or female?
Male—you have to light a fire under it to make it go, and of course it's full of hot air.

Web page—male or female?
Female—is always getting hit on.

Hammer—male or female?
Male—hasn't evolved much in 5000 years.

How are men like high heels?
They are easy to walk on once you get the hang of it.

Why do women need men?
Because vibrators can't take out the trash.

How many sensitive, honest men does it take to take out the trash?
Both of them.

Why don't women blink during foreplay?
Not enough time.

How does a man prove he is planning for the future?
He buys two cases of beer.

Why are blonde jokes so short?
So men can remember them.

Why is it difficult for women to find sensitive, available men?
They already have boyfriends.

What do you call a woman who knows where her husband is every night?
A widow.

When does a woman prefer a man's company?
When he owns one.

How did Pinocchio find out he was made of wood?
His hand caught on fire.

What do you call a virgin on a waterbed?
A cherry float.

What do you call a transvestite?
Someone who likes to eat, drink and be Mary.

If Hooters starts an airline, will their in-flight news be called **"Keeping Abreast"**?

New motto for Hooters Airlines in-flight meals: **"Just like Mom used to make"**

And will Hooters Airlines feature the Naked News Channel?

Divorce: Latin word meaning **"to yank a man's genitals through his wallet."**

I miss my ex, **but my aim is improving**.

Why does it take 100,000,000 sperm to fertilize one egg? **Because not one will stop and ask for directions.**

What does the Chicken Slogan: "It takes a tough man to make a tender chicken" mean in Spanish?
"It takes an aroused man to make a chicken affectionate."

Husband's note on fridge:
Doctor's office called.... says Pabst Beer is normal

What's the difference between a wife and a mistress?
45 pounds

What's the difference between a husband and a lover?
45 minutes

PRETTY BAD JOKES

Did you hear about the new Origami store?
It folded.

Give a man a fish and he'll eat for a day—Teach him to fish, and he'll drink beer for a lifetime.

You know you're old when you can remember when the Dead Sea just had a cold.

What do you take for an upset stomach when south of the border?
Mex-Lax

Did you catch a peek at the new Victoria's Secret model?
She was one haute tomato.

What does Fiat stand for?
Fix It Again, Tony

Did you hear about the new Goodyear Tires blow-out sale?

What do you call a cookbook for shoe leather?
Chicken Soup for the Sole

If airlines are going to charge for meals, should gas stations charge for bathrooms?

And why are locks put on gas station bathrooms?
So no one will break in and clean them.

If airlines charge for meals, should cabbies charge for fresh air?

There are three kinds of people: those who can count, and those who can't.

To all you virgins—thanks for nothing.

Always keep your words soft and sweet, in case you have to eat them.

Elephant—A mouse built to government specifications.

I love cooking with wine—Occasionally I put it in the food.

Did you hear about the psychic who was expelled for cheating? **He looked into the soul of the boy sitting next to him.**

Those are my principles—
If you don't like them,
I'll get others...

There's a new play
opening called *Urinetown*
—Is *Colostomy: The
Musical* far off?

If at first you don't
succeed, so much for
sky-diving.

Work is the curse of
the drinking class.

I'm a drinker with
writing problems.

I want to live forever,
or die in the process.

I started with nothing,
and I still have most
of it.

I don't ever remember
being absent-minded.

The only difference
between a rut and a
grave is depth.

The next time you wave, use all your fingers.

That man had the intelligence of three men: Larry, Moe and Curley.

Despite the high cost of living, it remains very popular.

Remember: Six out of eight people make up 75% of the population.

SIZE MATTERS

1000 aches equal a mega-hurtz.

One unit of laryngitis equals one hoarsepower.

2000 mockingbirds equal Two Kilomockingbirds.

One kilogram of falling figs equals one fig Newton.

1000 grams of wet socks equals one literhosen.

One millionth of 1 fish equals one microfish.

8 nickels equals 2 paradigms.

SMART SIGNS

No Trespassing Without
Permission

Open Seven Days a Week
and Weekends

Sign outside travel agency:
Why don't you go away?

Written on child's cough
medicine: Do not operate
car after taking

Written on Christmas tree
lights: For indoor or outdoor
use only

REJECTED KIDS BOOK TITLES

*Harry Potter and the Tube
of K-Y Jelly*

*Harry Potter and His
Pal From Sing Sing*

*Harry Potter and the Chamber
of Viagra*

Dr. Seuss' The Cat in the Burlap Sack

Jeans and Spleens

Green Eggs and Crack

Horton Hires a Ho

Simpson Cuts the Brake Lines

Curious George Flips Off a Cop

Pete Townshend's Playhouse

Dad's New Wife, Jack

*The Boy Who Died From Eating
All His Vegetables*

BOOKS THAT DIDN'T MAKE IT

Classic Books I Have Cherished
—A. Nicole Smith

Meals I Have Passed By
—Rosie O' Donnell

My Favorite Persons of Color
—Trent Lott

Why I Love THE GREAT SOCIETY
—Jesse Helms

Fans Who Have Loved Me
—Simon Cowell

The One-Armed Man Did It
—O. J. Simpson

Childcare is a Snap
—Michael Jackson

The Kids are Alright
—P. Townsend

Sit By Me at the Movies
—P. Wee Herman

REAL LIFE HEADLINES

(WE COULDN'T MAKE THIS STUFF UP.)

"Hurricane Rips Through Graveyard: Hundreds Feared Dead"

"Drunk Gets Nine Months In Violin Case"

"Farmer Bill Dies In House"

"Iraqi Head Seeks Arms"

"Is There A Ring Of Debris Around Uranus?"

"Kids Make Nutritious Snacks"

"Soviet Union Finds Dwarfs In Short Supply"

"Number Of High School Dropouts Cut In Half"

"Wheat Farmers Feed Rumor Mill"

"Will Moon Expose Its Secrets?"

"New Vaccine May Contain Rabies"

"Man Loses Ear—Waives Hearing"

"Thief Caught With Clock—
Faces Time"

"Several Pieces Of Rock
Hudson Sold At Auction"

"Sex Ed Delayed—Teachers
Request Training"

"Include Children When
Baking Cookies"

"Stud Tires Out"

"Prostitute Appeals To Pope"

"Teacher Strikes Idle Kids"

"Reagan Wins On Budget, But More Lies Ahead"

"Squad Helps Dog Bite Victims"

"Plane Too Close To Ground, Crash Probe Told"

"Miners Refuse To Work After Death"

"Juvenile Court To Try Shooting Defendant"
"Two Soviet Ships Collide, One Dies"

"Killer Sentenced To Die For Second Time In Ten Years"

"War Dims Hope For Peace"

"If Strike Isn't Settled
Quickly, May Last"

"Couple Slain—Police
Suspect Homicide"

"Red Tape Holds Up
New Bridge"

"Man Struck By Lightning
Faces Battery Charge"

"Police Campaign To
Run Down Jaywalkers"

"British Left Waffles
On Falklands"

"Clinton Places Dickey
In Gore's Hands"

"Alzheimers Center
Prepares For *An Affair To
Remember*"

"Fried Chicken Cooked
In Microwave Wins Trip"

"Deer Kills 23,000"

"Gators To Face Seminoles
With Peters Out"

"Bargain Basement Upstairs"

"Gas Cloud Clears Out Taco Bell"

"Legislator Wants Tougher Death Penalty"

STILL MORE JOKES

This is not a book to be tossed aside lightly: **It should be thrown with great force.**

The pen is mightier than the sword, and easier to write with.

You may be working too hard... if you stare at an orange juice container because it says **CONCENTRATE**.

Sure, there have been deaths in boxing, but none of them serious.

You may be working too hard...if you stop to see what direction the water swirls when you flush.

You may be a geek...
if you get out your old slide rule to practice, just in case.

Critics are to movies what dogs are to lampposts.

Why does a sorority girl close her eyes during sex? **So she can fantasize about shopping.**

What's the difference between a cheerleading squad and a circus? **A circus is a cunning array of stunts.**

How do crazy people go through forests? **Psycho paths**

How do you make
holy water?
Boil the hell out of it.

What do prisoners call
each other on?
Cell phones

What do you call
someone else's cheese?
Nacho cheese

What do you call
Santa's helpers?
Subordinate clauses

What do you call four hombres in quicksand?
Quatro sinko

What do you get from a fussy cow?
Spoiled milk

What is a zebra?
25 sizes bigger than an "A" bra

What is at the bottom of the ocean and twitches?
A nervous wreck

What is the difference
between roast beef
and pea soup?
Anyone can roast beef.

You might be an
engineer... if you use
a bullet format for
your grocery list.

You might be a defense
contractor... if you can
neither "confirm nor
deny" how your day
went at work.

Where do you find
virgin wool?
Ugly sheep

What is another name
for pickled bread?
Dill dough

Why don't blind people
like sky-diving?
**It scares the hell out
of the dogs.**

Verbal contract:
not worth the paper
it's written on.

OXY-MORONS?

Act naturally

Found missing

Resident alien

Good grief

Sanitary landfill

Legally drunk

Small crowd

Business ethics

Soft rock

Butt head

Military intelligence

Sweet sorrow

Now, then

Synthetic natural gas

Taped live

Clearly misunderstood

Peace force

Extinct life

Plastic glasses

Terribly pleased

Political science

Tight slacks

Pretty ugly

12-ounce pound cake

Exact estimate

Microsoft Works

JOKES FOR COTTON-HEADS

You know you're getting older when your wild oats become prunes and all-bran.

Age is a question of mind over matter: **If you don't mind, it don't matter.**

Time is a great healer, but a lousy beautician.

1970: Hoping for a BMW
2000: Hoping for a BM

1970: Grateful Dead
2000: Dr. Kevorkian

1970: Whatever
2000: Depends

CLEVER QUOTES

Dan Quayle:
"I love California—I practically grew up in Phoenix."

Raquel Welch:
"I was asked to come to Chicago, because it's one of our 52 states."

Ivana Trump:
"Fiction writing is great—you can make up almost anything."

Lee Iacocca:
"We've got to ask ourselves...How much clean air do we need?"

Christie Brinkley:
"I wish my butt did not go sideways, but I guess I'll have to face that."

Marion Barry:
"Outside of the killings, D.C. has one of the lowest crime rates in the country."

Mariah Carey
(on seeing starving children commercial on TV):
"I'd love to be skinny like that, but without all the flies and death and stuff."

FAMOUS LAST WORDS

Jack Warner:
"Who the hell wants to hear actors talk?"

Ernie Kovacs:
"TV is a medium—neither rare nor well-done."

Ivana Trump:
"Don't get mad, get everything."

Gary Hart:
"I'll take the blonde, you take the brunette."

I've been accused of vulgarity—that's total bullshit.

SHORT JOKES

Danny DeVito....no, that's not a short joke.

Napoleon: no, no, no...

PHILO-SOPHIC JOKES

If flying is so safe, why do they call the airport the "terminal"?

If the Jaguars are the Jags, the Buccaneers the Bucs; then what are the Titans?

If four out of five people suffer from diarrhea, does that mean one enjoys it?

If croutons are stale
bread, why do they come
in airtight packages?

Why does sour
cream come with
an expiration date?

If Fed Ex and UPS
combine, will they be
Fed-UP?

If you eat something
and no one sees you,
does it have calories?

Do radioactive cats have
18 half-lives?

Great Questions in Life:
Would the ocean be
deeper without sponges?

When cemeteries raise
burial costs, do they
blame it on the cost
of living?

Why is lemon juice made
with artificial flavor, and
dishwashing liquid made
with real lemons?

Why is the man who invests your money called a broker?

Why is it necessary to nail down the lid of a coffin?

If you had everything, where would you put it?

Why are there signs for illiteracy?

Why do Kamikaze pilots wear helmets?

If it is H2O inside the fire hydrant, what is on the outside? K9P

Why isn't phonetic spelled the way it sounds?

Why is there an interstate in Hawaii?

If the black box is so safe, why isn't the whole plane made of that stuff?

Do you need a silencer to shoot a mime?

Ever imagined a world with no hypothetical situations?

How does the guy on the snowplow get to work?

If 7 Eleven's are open 24 hours/7 days a week, why are there locks on the door?

If a cow laughs, will milk come out of his nose?

Why are there Braille dots on drive-up ATMs?

If all is not lost, where is it?

Do illiterate people enjoy alphabet soup?

Is half of a large intestine a semi-colon?

How do they get deer to cross at the yellow signs?

Why do we drive on a parkway, and park on a driveway?

Why is it when we get lost in a car, we turn down the radio?

If corn oil is from corn, where does baby oil come from?

Why do they insist on using a new needle to give deadly injections?

What's another word
for thesaurus?

Why is the word
'abbreviation' so long?

What was the greatest
thing before sliced bread?

Do hungry crows have
ravenous appetites?

Is it possible to be
totally partial?

If a parsley farmer is sued, do they garnish his wages?

If a Stealth bomber crashes in the woods, does it make a sound?

If a tortoise loses his shell, is it homeless?

When it rains, why don't sheep shrink?

Do vegetarians eat animal crackers?

CONDOM AD CAMPAIGNS THAT WERE NEVER USED

It will be sweeter
if you wrap your peter

If you go into heat,
wrap your meat

Especially in December,
wrap your member

ALL TIME WORST PICK-UP LINES

You want to see a hold
I learned in prison?

Hey baby, what's
your sign?
Do Not Enter

I just love slasher
movies, don't you?

BLONDE
JOKES

That blonde is depriving
a village somewhere of
an idiot.

This blonde should
go far, and the sooner
she starts, the better.

This blonde got into
the gene pool when the
lifeguard wasn't looking.

That blonde has a warm
personality and a room
temperature IQ.

That blonde had a photographic memory with the lens cap still on.

That blonde donated her brain to science before she was finished with it.

That blonde fell out of the family tree.

If you gave a blonde a penny for her thoughts, you'd get change.

If you stand close enough
to that blonde, you can
hear the ocean.

It's hard to believe
that blonde beat out
1,000,000 other sperm.

Some drink from the
fountain of knowledge,
she only gargled.

The wheel is turning but
the hamster is dead.

That young lady has delusions of adequacy.

She set low personal standards and then consistently failed to achieve them.

REJECTED STATE SLOGANS

Wisconsin—Come cut
the cheese

Florida—November is learn
how to vote month

Hawaii—Hila toku
mia shiami (death to
mainlanders, but leave
your money)

Illinois—Isn't it time you
tried our rest areas?

Kansas—Come see the
world's largest group of
Kansans

Kentucky—5 million people—15 last names

Michigan—First line of defense from Canada

Minnesota—10,000 lakes/ 10,000,000 mosquitoes

Mississippi—Come feel better about your own state

Montana—We put the fun in fundamentalism

Nevada—Whores! Poker!

New Mexico—For sale
by owner—best offer

Oklahoma—Like the play,
only no singing

South Carolina—Remember
the Civil War? We never
actually surrendered.

Tennessee—Come see
the shed where Al Gore
invented the Internet

Utah—Imagine 27 wives
asking if they look fat.

Washington—People will pay
$4.00 for a cup of coffee!!!

West Virginia—One big,
happy family!

Wyoming—Scared sheep are
everywhere

JOKES
IN OTHER
LANGUAGES

Why are they called the Chevy Nova Awards when "No Va" in Spanish means "no go"?

"Got Milk?" in Spanish: "Are you lactating?"

Coors "Turn it Loose" campaign in Spanish: "Suffers from diarrhea."

Electrolux's ad slogan in Scandanavian: "Nothing sucks like an Electrolux."

WHY DID THE CHICKEN CROSS THE ROAD?

(FAMOUS ANSWERS)

To die. In the rain.
—Ernest Hemingway

To steal a job from a decent,
hardworking American.
—Pat Buchanan

To find the real killer.
—O.J. Simpson

To boldly go where no
chicken had gone before.
—James T. Kirk

It depends on what
you mean by "chicken."
—W. J. Clinton

You mean I missed one?
—Colonel Sanders

"AND THE JOKES JUST KEEP ON COMING" JOKES

A boat of lawyers capsized in the sea, but the sharks refused to eat them. Why?
Professional courtesy

What do you call 2.2 miles of surgical tubing at Harvard University Hospital?
One I. V. League

99% of all lawyers give the rest a bad name.

Atheism is a non-prophet organization.

My first job was in
an orange juice factory,
but I couldn't concentrate,
and got canned. So I tried
working in a muffler
factory and got exhausted.
They moved me to
automotive, but I got
tired. Then I worked
at a coffee shop, but it
was the same old grind.

Actually, I'm not a
vegetarian because I
like animals, it's because
I hate vegetables.

PARTING SHOTS

Monica didn't work
for Clinton's re-election
campaign—**She just paid
it lip service.**

Why did Clara Harris
run over her husband
in a Mercedes?
**The Land Rover was
in the shop.**

Does Clara Harris think
her husband will forgive
her for what she did?
**She isn't sure, but says
she will run it by him.**

Does Clara Harris think this unfortunate accident will affect her future? **No. She feels it is just a bump in the road.**

President Bush feels he deserved his election win **—Al Gore had only written one book, and Bush had read at least two.**

If Kelly Ripa married mobster John Dillinger and kept her name, would she be **Mrs. Jack D. Ripa?**

Did congressman
James Traficant think
he would have to do time
for his indiscretion?
**No. He was hoping
they would just sweep
it under the rug.**

What do Anna Nicole
Smith and *Star Wars*
have in common?
**They were both conceived
long ago, in a Galaxy 500
far, far away.**

Michael Jackson, who assured reporters today that he has not had facial surgery, seems to have a shrinking nose— **In related news, Pinocchio's nose seems to be getting bigger.**

Answer: Rhett Butler. Michael Jackson's nose. The president of Clonaid. **Question: Name a rake, a mistake, and a fruitcake.**

Answer: A set of Goodyears.
A Ford Expedition.
Osama bin Laden's cave.
**Question: Name three
things that blow up often.**

What do Michael Jackson
and lobster fishermen
have in common?
They both love new buoys.

POP QUIZ

(TO SEE IF YOU WERE PAYING ATTENTION.)

1. How were Al Qaeda prisoners punished in Cuban prison camps?

a) a year of hard labor

b) a month of solitary confinement

c) nightly screenings of *ISHTAR*

2. Losing contestants on *Fear Factor* were forced to:

a) eat horse tail

b) eat man-sized grub worms

c) spend a week with Simon Cowell

3) What is the significance of the figure: 5 billion dollars?

a) amount of trade deficit with China

b) sum spent on Paula Jones's nose

c) money lost on *PLUTO NASH*

4. What is the BattleStar Galactica?

a) a fictional movie ship

b) futuristic model for space ships

c) part of the naval carrier group headed by the USS A. NICOLE SMITH

5. What do you call it when Leona Helmsley, Martha Stewart and Wynona Ryder get together?

a) a promo for a new talk show
b) a rehearsal for *The Vagina Monologues*
c) cell block H

6. "Through A Glass Darkly" is:

a) a book of sensitive poetry
b) about the making of the Hubble Telescope
c) Trent Lott's new tell-all

7. "My Life With Lincoln" is:
a) a Confederate spy's diary
b) Mary Todd Lincoln's saucy confidential
c) Jesse Helm's autobiography

8. The only man-made object visible from the space shuttle is:
a) the pyramids at Giza
b) The Great Wall of China
c) James Traficant's hair

9) A black hole is:
a) a celestial body of nothingness
b) Anna Nicole Smith's bookbag
c) health benefits package at WorldCom

10. Marie Antoinette was:

a) a beautiful French monarch
b) a classmate of Shirley MacLaine
c) inspiration for Mrs. Kenneth Lay's "let them eat cake" speech

All test results are confidential, original and definitely not the property of major league baseball—

Goodnight, Mrs. Calabash, wherever you are!!

B. GUTT
Beverly Hills, California